Basic Skills

MW01716459

Math Fact Families

Grade 4

By
Cherie Walters

Cover Artist
Matthew Van Zomeren

Inside Illustrations by
Marty Bucella

Published by Instructional Fair • TS Denison
an imprint of

McGraw-Hill Children's Publishing

About the Author

Mrs. Cherie Walters has taught high school, middle school, and for the last fourteen years, has been teaching at the elementary level. She loves nearly everything to do with teaching! When not in the classroom, Cherie enjoys traveling, biking, snorkeling, writing, and spending time with her husband Rich and son Max.

Dedication

Mrs. Cherie Walters would like to dedicate this book to "the two most wonderful men in my life, my husband Rich and my son Max."

Credits

Author: Cherie Walters
Illustrator: Marty Bucella
Cover Graphics: Matthew Van Zomeren
Project Director/Editor: Mary Rose Hassinger
Editors: Christopher Kjaer, Elizabeth Flikkema
Graphic Layout: Tracy L. Wesorick

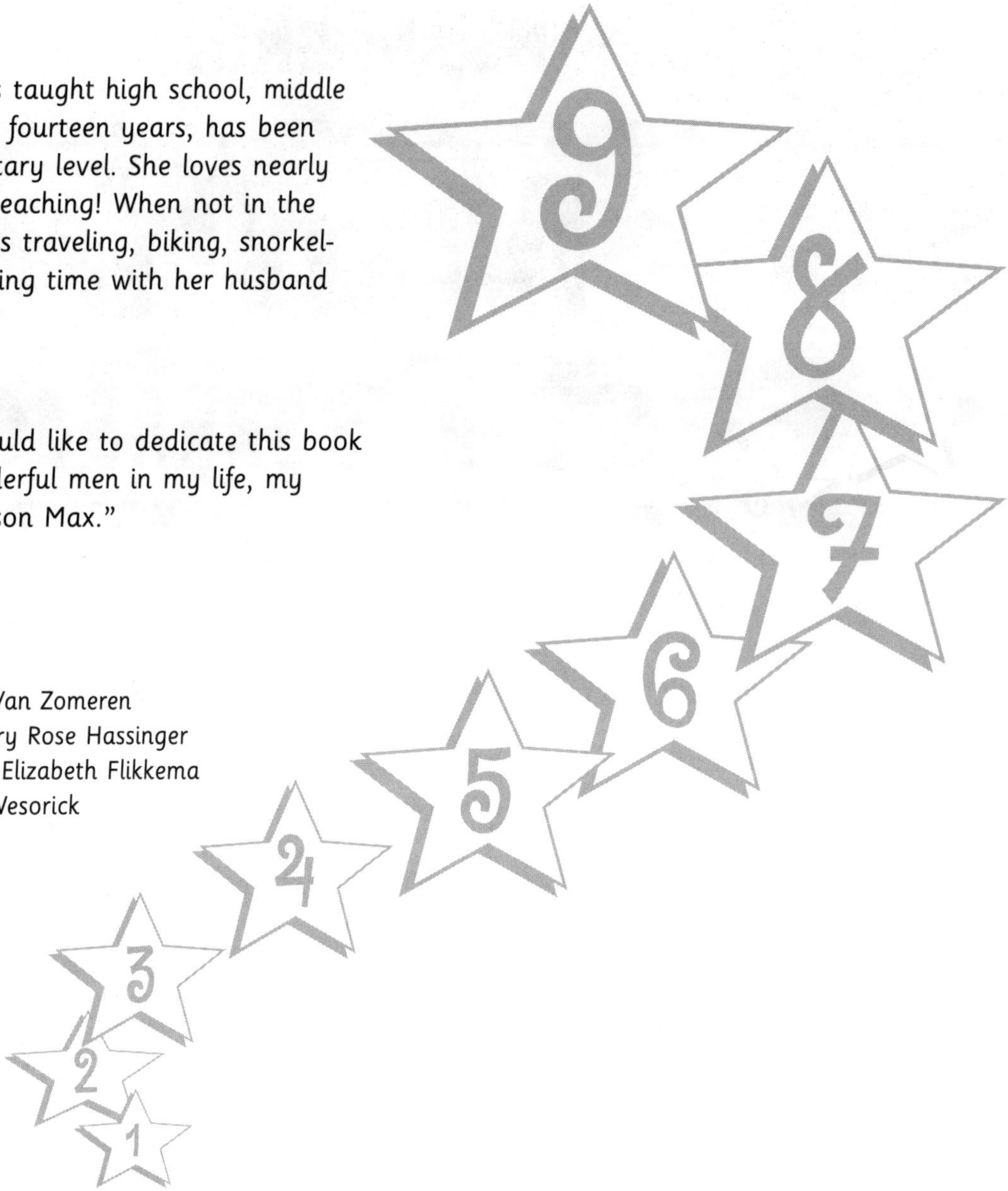

McGraw-Hill
Children's Publishing

A Division of The McGraw-Hill Companies

Published by Instructional Fair • TS Denison
An imprint of McGraw-Hill Children's Publishing
Copyright © 2001 McGraw-Hill Children's Publishing

Limited Reproduction Permission: Permission to duplicate these materials is limited to the person for whom they are purchased. Reproduction for an entire school or school district is unlawful and strictly prohibited.

Send all inquiries to:
McGraw-Hill Children's Publishing
3195 Wilson Drive NW
Grand Rapids, Michigan 49544

All Rights Reserved • Printed in the United States of America

Math Fact Families—grade 4
ISBN: 0-7424-0097-2

About the Book

Teaching and learning math strategies at any level can be a challenging and often frustrating experience. *Math Fact Families* for grade 4 briefly reviews addition and subtraction and introduces multiplication and division fact families. The instruction of such strongly related skills in this innovative format will make learning basic computation a successful and rewarding experience. From the reviewing of the addition and subtraction to the use of fact families for multiplication and division and other operations, and the importance of the family member position, this unique method of instruction is very user-friendly. The use of the familiar family theme to teach number combinations (e.g., 2 • 3 • 6 to teach 2 x 3 = 6, 3 x 2 = 6, 6 ÷ 2 = 3, 6 ÷ 3 = 2) is easily understood, as is the use of the terms *parent* for the largest number in the family, and *children* for the two smaller numbers.

Math Fact Families is a great source of organized, logical materials that is hard to find anywhere else. These lessons will help strengthen the students' computation skills as well as prepare them for the higher-level thinking that follows full understanding of the basics.

Table of Contents

Name________________________

addition/subtraction

Math Fact Families

The three numbers that make a math sentence are part of a fact family. A family is made up of two smaller numbers, which are the *children*, and a bigger number, which is the *parent*. Here is a fact family.

You've just met the 3 • 4 • 7 family. The 3 • 4 • 7 family can be seen in four different math sentences.

You see it in addition... $4 + 3 = 7$ and $3 + 4 = 7$.

And you see it in subtraction... $7 - 3 = 4$ and $7 - 4 = 3$.

Circle the addition and subtraction statements that are a part of each fact family.

1. 7 • 8 • 15	2. 6 • 7 • 13	3. 8 • 9 • 17	4. 6 • 8 • 14
7 + 8 = 15	6 + 1 = 7	17 – 7 = 10	6 + 7 = 13
7 + 8 15	7 + 6 13	8 + 9 17	8 + 6 14
8 – 7 = 1	7 – 5 = 2	8 – 1 = 7	16 – 8 = 8
7 – 4 3	13 – 6 7	17 – 9 8	14 – 6 8

Name______________________

addition/subtraction

Look to the Parent

A parent is someone who helps us in many ways. In fact families, the parent helps us, too. By recognizing the parent in a math problem, you can tell what kind of problem it is.

By recognizing the parent, you can tell what kind of operation is involved in the math problem. Follow these suggestions.

In an addition problem, the parent is always the answer.

child + child = parent

```
  child
+ child
-------
 parent
```

In a subtraction problem, the parent is always at the top or beginning of a problem.

parent – child = child

```
 parent
– child
-------
  child
```

Circle the parent in these problems, then put a plus or minus sign in each circle.

1.
```
   5
○  9
----
  14
```

2.
```
   9
○  5
----
  14
```

3.
```
  14
○  9
----
   5
```

4.
```
  14
○  5
----
   9
```

5. 9 ○ 5 = 14

6. 5 ○ 9 = 14

7. 14 ○ 5 = 9

8. 14 ○ 9 = 5

Name________________________

addition/subtraction

Addition/Subtraction Flash Cards

Cut apart the flash cards on the dotted lines. Use the cards for oral practice. Mix the cards and cover one corner with your hand. Name the hidden number. Add if the parent is hidden. Subtract if a child is hidden. Memorize the members of each fact family.

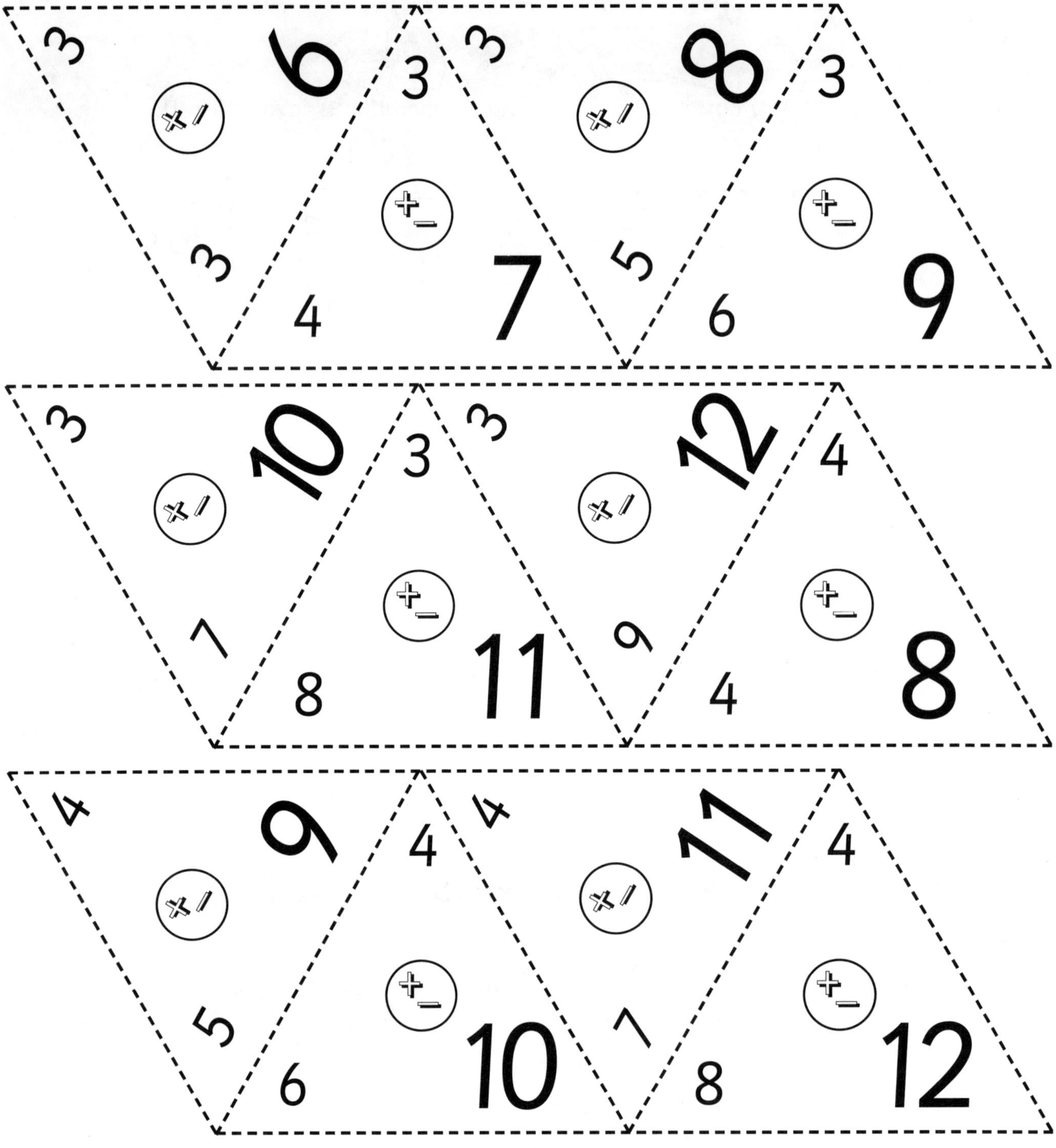

© Instructional Fair • TS Denison

Name________________________

addition/subtraction

Addition/Subtraction Flash Cards

Cut apart the flash cards on the dotted lines. Use the cards for oral practice. Mix the cards and cover one corner with your hand. Name the hidden number. Add if the parent is hidden. Subtract if a child is hidden. Memorize the members of each fact family.

4, 9, 13 (×/÷)	5, 5, 10 (+/−)	5, 6, 11 (×/÷)	5, 7, 12 (+/−)
5, 8, 13 (×/÷)	5, 9, 14 (+/−)	6, 6, 12 (×/÷)	6, 7, 13 (+/−)
6, 8, 14 (×/÷)	6, 9, 15 (+/−)	7, 7, 14 (×/÷)	7, 8, 15 (+/−)

Name________________

Addition/Subtraction Flash Cards

Cut apart the flash cards on the dotted lines. Use the cards for oral practice. Mix the cards and cover one corner with your hand. Name the hidden number. Add if the parent is hidden. Subtract if a child is hidden. Memorize the members of each fact family.

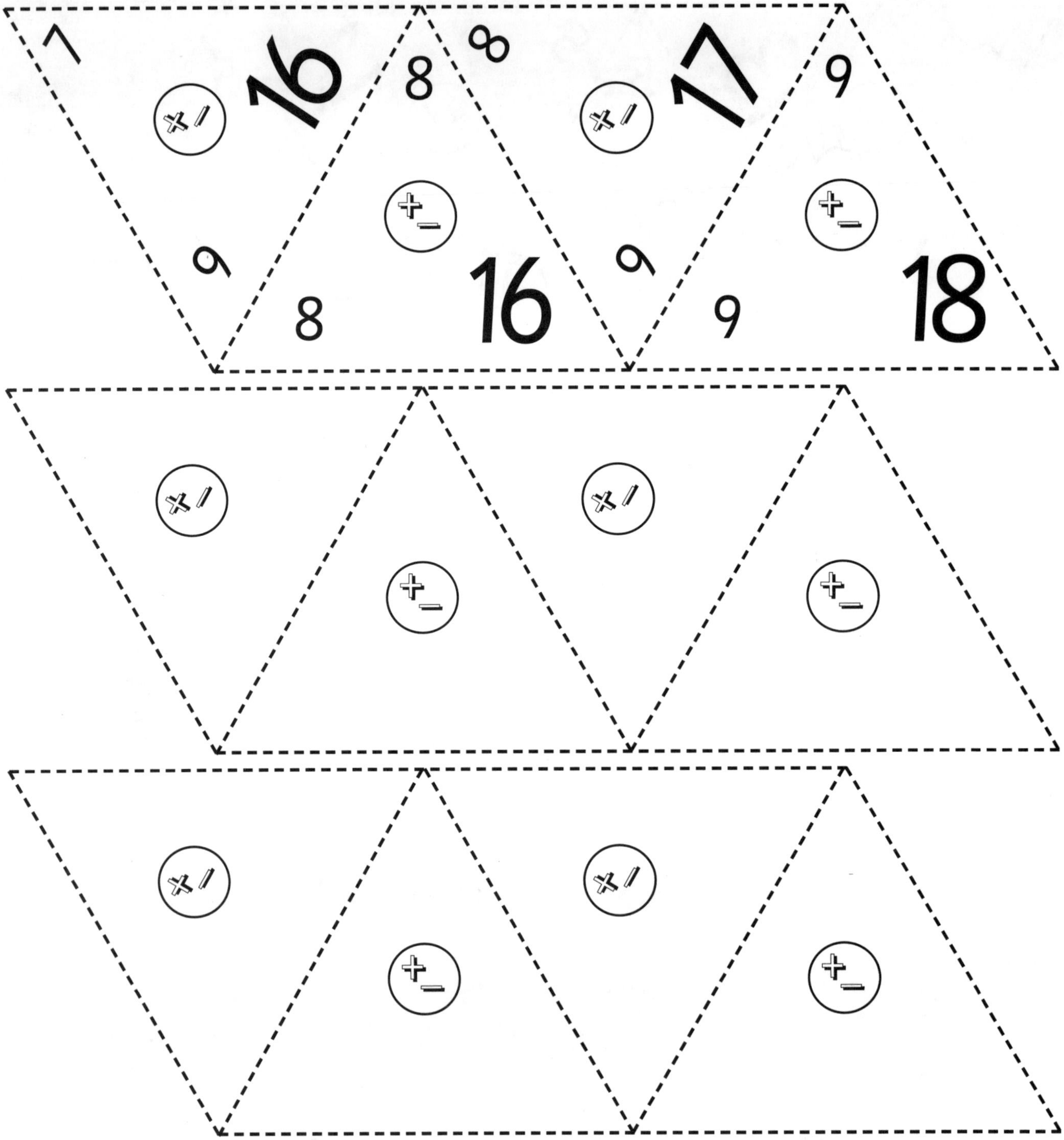

Name________________________

addition/subtraction

Soaring Through Threes

Three is the smallest child in these fact families.

3 • 3 • 6   3 • 4 • 7   3 • 5 • 8

3 • 6 • 9   3 • 7 • 10   3 • 8 • 11   3 • 9 • 12

Circle the clouds that hold facts that belong to the fact families below the planes.

1. 3 • 3

2. 3 • 8

3. 3 • 5

4. 3 • 4

5. 3 • 7

6. 3 • 6

7. 3 • 9

Name________________________

addition/subtraction

Fours All the Way

Four is the smallest child in these fact families.

4 • 4 • 8   4 • 5 • 9   4 • 6 • 10   4 • 7 • 11   4 • 8 • 12   4 • 9 • 13

In the boxes, find and circle the numerals that make a fact family with four as the smallest child. Write the fact family below the box. The first one is done for you.

1.

14	8	4
4	10	16
17	19	73

4 • 4 • 8

2.

21	26	4
13	28	29
18	17	9

____

3.

11	19	19
29	7	13
41	21	4

____

4.

6	19	11
33	17	12
4	28	10

____

5.

9	16	9
72	14	8
4	9	5

____

6.

4	12	8
99	73	74
75	13	11

____

It's a Fact

Name________________________

addition/subtraction

These fact families have 5 and 6 as the smallest child.

5 • 5 • 10   5 • 6 • 11   5 • 7 • 12   5 • 8 • 13   5 • 9 • 14

6 • 6 • 12   6 • 7 • 13   6 • 8 • 14   6 • 9 • 15

Working diagonally, circle fact families with 5s and 6s as the smallest child.

6	5	8	6	6	5	4	1	5	2	6	4	5	11	7
6	8	6	4	3	7	5	3	9	8	7	7	1	9	6
3	7	14	11	5	1	13	10	2	9	13	2	13	2	14
5	7	6	0	0	7	6	7	0	0	7	1	5	9	3
6	5	4	8	6	5	12	6	1	5	8	1	4	8	3
6	3	10	5	14	2	3	2	6	4	6	9	5	4	13
1	6	9	6	7	7	1	8	9	12	3	11	1	9	0
7	5	1	9	8	4	6	5	8	6	4	5	6	2	14
6	9	7	2	0	3	5	6	5	7	9	0	9	9	7
9	0	6	12	3	1	9	1	12	8	2	14	4	4	15

© Instructional Fair • TS Denison

Name____________________

addition/subtraction

Surfing Through 7, 8, and 9

These math fact families feature 7, 8, and 9 as the smallest child.

7 • 7 • 14	7 • 8 • 15	7 • 9 • 16
8 • 8 • 16	8 • 9 • 17	9 • 9 • 18

Use the above fact families to help answer the following problems.

1. $8 + 7$	2. $7 + 7$	3. $16 - 8$	4. $17 - 8$
5. $9 + 9$	6. $9 + 8$	7. $16 - 9$	8. $14 - 7$
9. $8 + 8$	10. $7 + 9$	11. $17 - 9$	12. $16 - 8$
13. $7 + 8$	14. $7 + 7$	15. $18 - 9$	16. $15 - 7$
17. $9 + 7$	18. $8 + 9$	19. $15 - 8$	20. $16 - 7$

© Instructional Fair • TS Denison

Name________________________

addition/subtraction

Chart What You've Learned

Keep track of the addition and subtraction facts you know. Notice the children are outside the chart and the parents are inside. Follow the column and row to match two children and write in the parent. You'll notice the same family is found twice on the chart. That is because (3 + 4), (4 + 3), (7 – 3), and (7 – 4) all come from the same family. Once you know the family, you know the answers to four problems.

The 3 • 4 • 7 family has been done for you.

+	1	2	3	4	5	6	7	8	9
1									
2									
3				7					
4			7						
5									
6									
7									
8									
9									

Name______________________

addition/subtraction

Focus on the Bigger Picture

Fact families can be found in larger math problems.

To solve this problem $\begin{array}{r} 64 \\ +\ 33 \\ \hline \end{array}$ begin in the ones column. $\begin{array}{r|l} 6 & 4 \\ +\ 3 & 3 \\ \hline & 7 \end{array}$ Remember math fact family 3 • 4 • 7 (4 + 3 = 7)

Then solve the tens column. $\begin{array}{r|l} 6 & 4 \\ +\ 3 & 3 \\ \hline 9 & 7 \end{array}$ Remember math fact family 3 • 6 • 9 (6 + 3 = 9)

You've done it! $\begin{array}{r} 64 \\ +\ 33 \\ \hline 97 \end{array}$

Solve these 2-digit math equations. Add or subtract the ones column first, then the tens column. Name the fact families found in each problem. Two problems are done for you.

1. $\begin{array}{r} 34 \\ +43 \\ \hline 77 \end{array}$ 3 • 4 • 7 / 3 • 4 • 7

2. $\begin{array}{r} 68 \\ -\ 36 \\ \hline 32 \end{array}$ 2 • 6 • 8 / 3 • 3 • 6

3. $\begin{array}{r} 45 \\ +\ 54 \\ \hline \end{array}$ ___•___•___ / ___•___•___

4. $\begin{array}{r} 86 \\ -43 \\ \hline \end{array}$ ___•___•___ / ___•___•___

5. $\begin{array}{r} 53 \\ +\ 35 \\ \hline \end{array}$ ___•___•___ / ___•___•___

6. $\begin{array}{r} 88 \\ -\ 35 \\ \hline \end{array}$ ___•___•___ / ___•___•___

7. $\begin{array}{r} 99 \\ -43 \\ \hline \end{array}$ ___•___•___ / ___•___•___

8. $\begin{array}{r} 77 \\ -\ 34 \\ \hline \end{array}$ ___•___•___ / ___•___•___

9. $\begin{array}{r} 99 \\ -\ 47 \\ \hline \end{array}$ ___•___•___ / ___•___•___

Name____________________

addition/subtraction

Climbing Higher

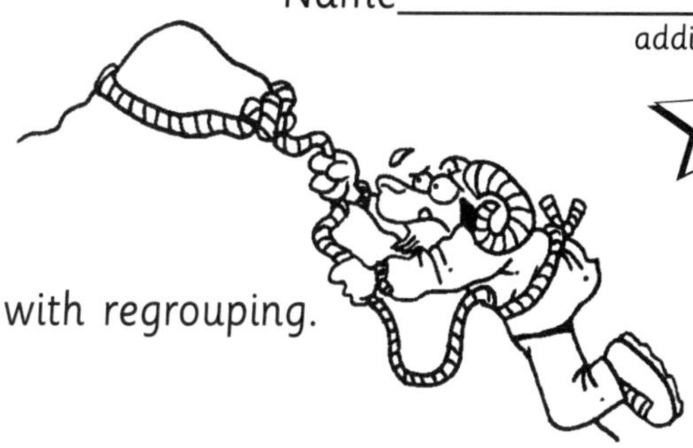

Fact families can be found in math problems with regrouping.

$$\begin{array}{r} 1 \\ 45 \\ +\ 37 \\ \hline 2 \end{array}$$

Remember math fact family 5 • 7 • 12 (5 + 7 = 12)

$$\begin{array}{r} 1 \\ 45 \\ +\ 37 \\ \hline 82 \end{array}$$

Remember math fact family 3 • 4 • 7 (4 + 3 = 7)

Step 1: Begin in the ones column.

Step 2: Since the answer is 12 and 12 has ones and a ten in it, place the ones portion of the answer below the line and put the tens portion on top of the tens column, where it can be added with the other tens.

Step 3: Look at the tens column.

Step 4: Add the 4 + 3 to make 7, then add the extra ten to make 8.

Follow the steps above. Add the ones column, then the tens column. Name the two fact families for each problem. The first one is done for you.

1. 38 + 43 = 81   3 • 4 • 7   3 • 8 • 11

2. 65 + 37   ___ • ___ • ___   ___ • ___ • ___

3. 45 + 55   ___ • ___ • ___   ___ • ___ • ___

4. 48 + 43   ___ • ___ • ___   ___ • ___ • ___

5. 59 + 35   ___ • ___ • ___   ___ • ___ • ___

6. 38 + 35   ___ • ___ • ___   ___ • ___ • ___

7. 46 + 47   ___ • ___ • ___   ___ • ___ • ___

8. 57 + 34   ___ • ___ • ___   ___ • ___ • ___

9. 58 + 37   ___ • ___ • ___   ___ • ___ • ___

Name________________________

addition/subtraction

Diving for Knowledge

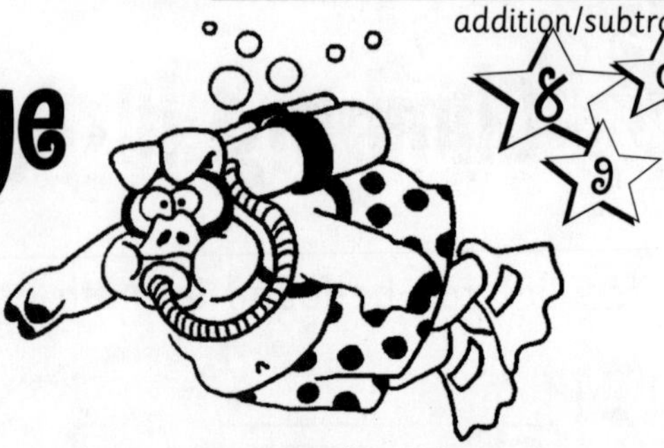

Fact families are found in 2-digit subtraction facts.

	Tens	Ones	
		15	Remember
	7 ~~8~~	~~5~~	math fact family
−	3	7	7 • 8 • 15
		8	(15 − 7 = 8)

Step 1: Begin with the ones column. Remember that the parent is always at the top of a subtraction problem and 5 is too small to be the parent of 7. Borrow a ten from the tens column and trade it for ten ones. Add them to the 5 ones. Now you have a parent—15.

	Tens	Ones	
		15	Remember
	7 ~~8~~	~~5~~	math fact family
−	3	7	3 • 4 • 7
	4	8	(7 − 3 = 4)

Step 2: Subtract 15 − 7 = 8. Place 8 in the answer.

Step 3: Solve the tens column. Remember you borrowed a ten and traded it to the ones column. Subtract 7 − 3 = 4.

The solution is 48.

Solve these subtraction problems. Name the two fact families for each statement. The first one is done for you.

1. 91 − 38 = 53 3 • 8 • 11 3 • 5 • 8

2. 75 − 37 ___•___•___ ___•___•___

3. 94 − 55 ___•___•___ ___•___•___

4. 81 − 43 ___•___•___ ___•___•___

5. 73 − 35 ___•___•___ ___•___•___

6. 90 − 35 ___•___•___ ___•___•___

7. 86 − 47 ___•___•___ ___•___•___

8. 72 − 32 ___•___•___ ___•___•___

9. 92 − 37 ___•___•___ ___•___•___

© Instructional Fair • TS Denison

Name____________________

addition/subtraction

Facts in Dollars and Decimals

Study the examples. Look for fact families in the equations and solve.

1 \$6.28 + 3.27 5	1 \$6.28 + 3.27 .55	1 \$6.28 + 3.27 \$9.55
Remember the fact family 7 • 8 • 15 (Carry the one.)	Remember the fact family 2 • 2 • 4 Then add the one. Don't forget to drop down the decimal.	Remember the fact family 3 • 6 • 9 Don't forget to drop down the dollar sign.

1. \$7.44 + 1.35
2. \$16.28 + 10.27
3. \$41.79 – 20.36
4. \$19.28 – 9.25
5. \$6.44 + 4.07
6. \$58.09 + 31.37
7. \$76.86 – 9.38
8. \$79.81 – 3.05
9. \$3.04 + 3.08
10. \$8.05 + 10.05
11. \$1.89 – 0.25
12. \$0.38 – 0.25
13. \$7.02 + 1.11
14. \$6.45 + 3.24
15. \$3.75 – 1.53
16. \$9.62 – 7.20

Name____________________

addition/subtraction

Starting with Algebra

Use your fact families to solve each math fact. Supply the member of the fact family that is represented by the X. The first one is done for you.

1. $3 + X = 6$ — $X = \underline{3}$
2. $7 - 4 = X$ — X = ___
3. $X + 6 = 15$ — X = ___
4. $5 + X = 11$ — X = ___
5. $18 - 9 = X$ — X = ___
6. $X + 9 = 13$ — X = ___
7. $15 - X = 8$ — X = ___
8. $X + 7 = 12$ — X = ___
9. $5 + X = 9$ — X = ___
10. $7 + X = 14$ — X = ___
11. $12 - 8 = X$ — X = ___
12. $16 - X = 7$ — X = ___
13. $16 - 8 = X$ — X = ___
14. $5 + X = 10$ — X = ___
15. $5 + X = 13$ — X = ___
16. $6 - X = 3$ — X = ___
17. $3 + 7 = X$ — X = ___
18. $5 + X = 8$ — X = ___
19. $12 - 9 = X$ — X = ___
20. $11 - X = 3$ — X = ___

Algebra Expert

Name________________________

addition/subtraction

Use fact families to solve each math fact. Supply the member of the fact family that is represented by the X. The first one is done for you.

1. 3 + X 3 X = <u>0</u>	2. 8 − X 4 X = ____	3. X + 6 11 X = ____	4. X + 7 12 X = ____	5. 8 − X 4 X = ____
6. 9 − 3 X X = ____	7. 15 − X 9 X = ____	8. 18 − 9 X X = ____	9. 10 − X 6 X = ____	10. X − 5 9 X = ____
11. 14 − X 8 X = ____	12. X + 7 14 X = ____	13. 8 + X 16 X = ____	14. 18 − X 9 X = ____	15. X + 3 6 X = ____
16. 11 − X 4 X = ____	17. X + 9 15 X = ____	18. X − 5 8 X = ____	19. X + 7 13 X = ____	20. X + 9 18 X = ____

Name____________________

Multiplying & Dividing Fact Families

Remember, in a fact family the two smaller numbers are the children, and the bigger number is the parent. This works in multiplication and division, too. The families we meet in multiplication and division are different from those we met in addition and subtraction.

This is the 3 • 4 • 12 family.

This family is seen in these multiplication problems.

$$4 \times 3 = 12 \qquad 3 \times 4 = 12$$

Here it is in division problems.

$$12 \div 3 = 4 \qquad 12 \div 4 = 3$$

In each box, circle the multiplication and division problems matching the fact families indicated.

1. 2 • 8 • 16	2. 1 • 5 • 5	3. 4 • 6 • 24	4. 6 • 8 • 48
$8 \times 2 = 16$	$5 \times 5 = 25$	$6 \times 6 = 36$	$6 \times 7 = 13$
$\begin{array}{r} 4 \\ \underline{\times\ 2} \\ 8 \end{array}$	$\begin{array}{r} 25 \\ \underline{\times\ 5} \\ 125 \end{array}$	$\begin{array}{r} 3 \\ \underline{\times\ 6} \\ 18 \end{array}$	$\begin{array}{r} 8 \\ \underline{\times\ 6} \\ 48 \end{array}$
$8 \div 2 = 4$	$5 \div 1 = 5$	$10 + 6 = 16$	$16 \div 8 = 8$
$\begin{array}{r} 8 \\ 2\overline{)16} \end{array}$	$\begin{array}{r} 5 \\ 1\overline{)5} \end{array}$	$\begin{array}{r} 4 \\ 6\overline{)24} \end{array}$	$\begin{array}{r} 6 \\ 8\overline{)48} \end{array}$

© Instructional Fair • TS Denison

Name________________________

multiplication/division

Look to the Parent II

In fact families, the parent helps you. If you locate the parent in a multiplication or division problem, you can tell what operation is being used in the problem.

In multiplication problems the parent is always the answer.

$$\begin{array}{r} \text{child} \\ \underline{\times\ \text{child}} \\ \text{parent} \end{array} \qquad \text{child} \times \text{child} = \text{parent}$$

In division facts, the parent is either at the beginning of a horizontal division fact or it is the number inside the box.

$$\text{parent} \div \text{child} = \text{child} \qquad \begin{array}{r} \text{child} \\ \text{child}\overline{\big)\,\text{parent}} \end{array}$$

Circle the parent in each of these math facts.

1. $\begin{array}{r} 3 \\ \underline{\times\ 4} \\ 12 \end{array}$
2. $\begin{array}{r} 4 \\ \underline{\times\ 3} \\ 12 \end{array}$
3. $\begin{array}{r} 7 \\ \underline{\times\ 3} \\ 21 \end{array}$
4. $\begin{array}{r} 7 \\ \underline{\times\ 4} \\ 28 \end{array}$
5. $\begin{array}{r} 5 \\ \underline{\times\ 4} \\ 20 \end{array}$
6. $\begin{array}{r} 4 \\ 6\overline{\big)24} \end{array}$
7. $\begin{array}{r} 6 \\ 3\overline{\big)18} \end{array}$
8. $\begin{array}{r} 9 \\ 4\overline{\big)36} \end{array}$
9. $\begin{array}{r} 3 \\ 4\overline{\big)12} \end{array}$
10. $\begin{array}{r} 5 \\ 4\overline{\big)20} \end{array}$

Using the math facts above, write in the parents of these math sentences.

11. 3 x 4 = ____
12. 7 x 3 = ____
13. 5 x 4 = ____
14. ____ ÷ 4 = 6
15. ____ ÷ 3 = 6
16. ____ ÷ 4 = 9

Name________________________

multiplication/division

Multiplying & Dividing Flash Cards

Cut apart the flash cards on the dotted lines. Use the cards for oral practice. Mix the cards and cover one corner with your hand. Name the hidden number. Multiply if the parent is hidden. Divide if a child is hidden. Memorize the members of each fact family.

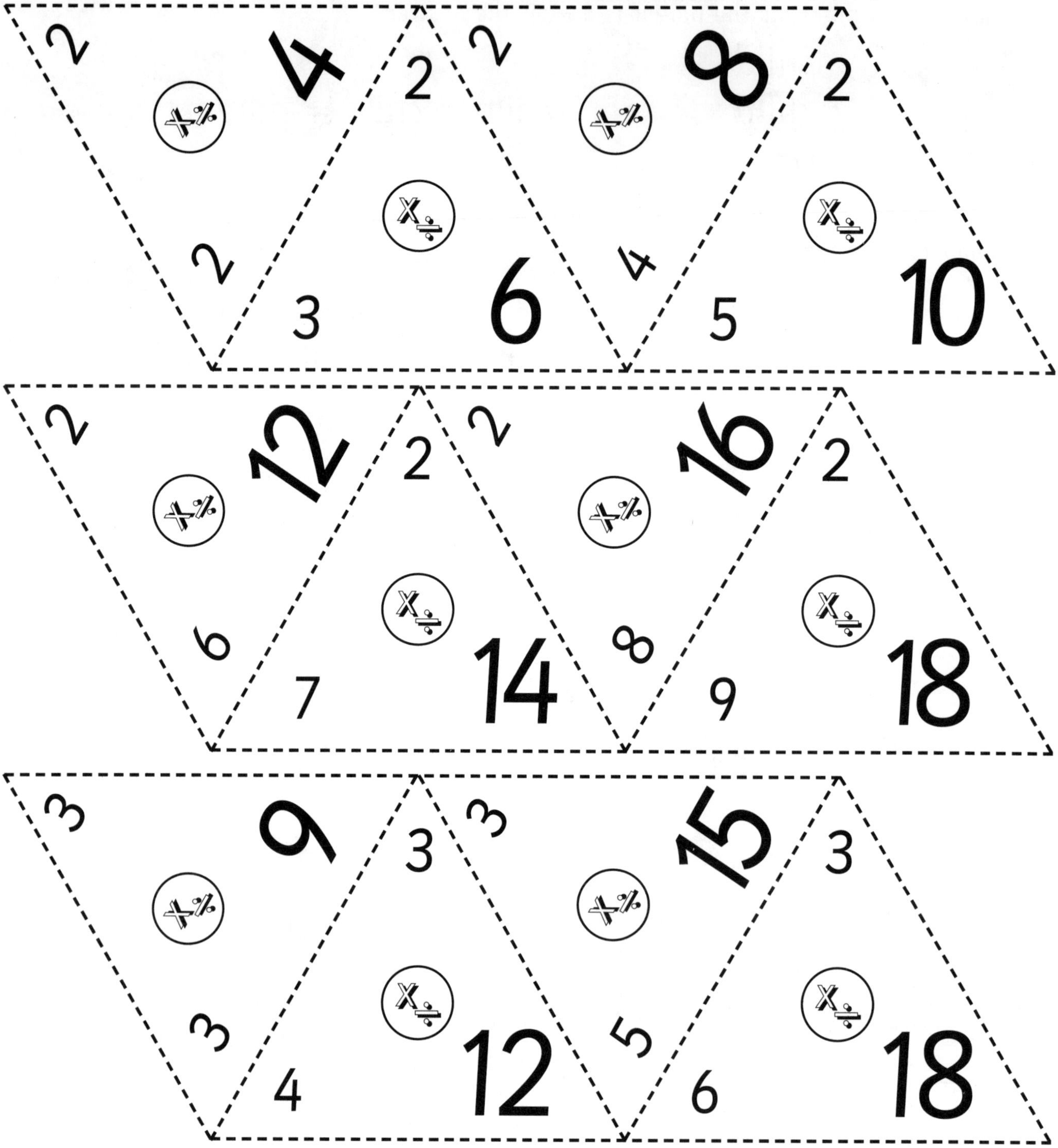

Name_______________________

multiplication/division

Flash Cards (cont.)

Cut apart the flash cards on the dotted lines. Use the cards for oral practice. Mix the cards and cover one corner with your hand. Name the hidden number. Multiply if the parent is hidden. Divide if a child is hidden. Memorize the members of each fact family.

3 7 21

3 8 24

3 9 27

4 4 16

4 5 20

4 6 24

4 7 28

4 8 32

4 9 32

5 5 25

5 6 30

5 7 35

Name____________________

multiplication/division

Flash Cards (cont.)

Cut apart the flash cards on the dotted lines. Use the cards for oral practice. Mix the cards and cover one corner with your hand. Name the hidden number. Multiply if the parent is hidden. Divide if a child is hidden. Memorize the members of each fact family.

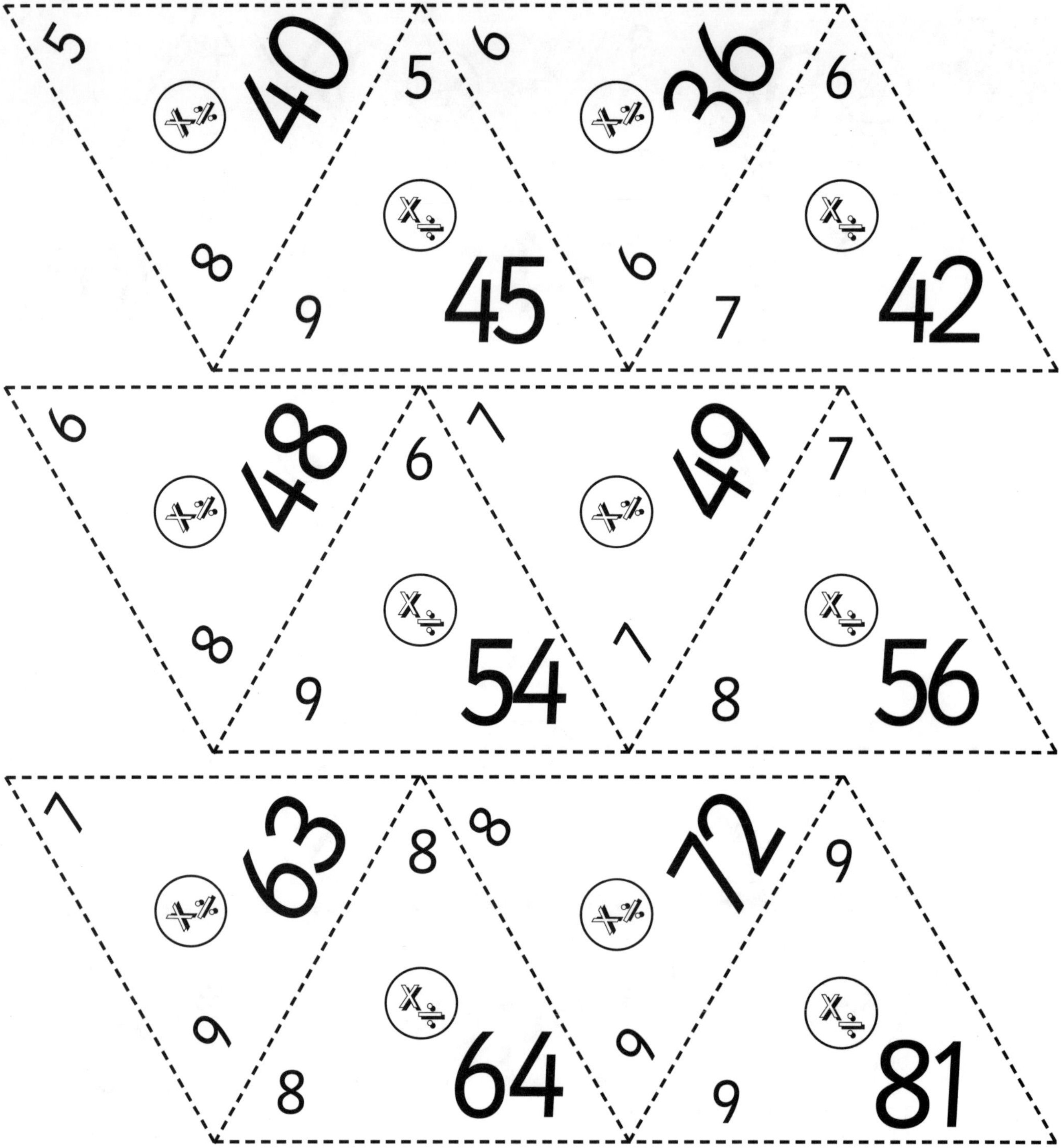

Name________________________

multiplication/division

Times 10, 11, & 12

Cut apart the flash cards on the dotted lines. Use the cards for oral practice. Mix the cards and cover one corner with your hand. Name the hidden number. Multiply if the parent is hidden. Divide if a child is hidden. Memorize the members of each fact family.

2, 10, 20

2, 11, 22

2, 12, 24

3, 10, 30

3, 11, 33

3, 12, 36

4, 10, 40

4, 11, 44

4, 12, 48

5, 10, 50

5, 11, 55

5, 12, 60

Name________________________

multiplication/division

Times 10, 11, & 12 (cont.)

Cut apart the flash cards on the dotted lines. Use the cards for oral practice. Mix the cards and cover one corner with your hand. Name the hidden number. Multiply if the parent is hidden. Divide if a child is hidden. Memorize the members of each fact family.

6 10 60

6 11 66

6 12 72

7 10 70

7 11 77

7 12 84

8 10 80

8 11 88

8 12 96

9 10 90

9 11 99

9 12 108

Name________________________

multiplication/division

Times 10, 11, & 12 (cont.)

Cut apart the flash cards on the dotted lines. Use the cards for oral practice. Mix the cards and cover one corner with your hand. Name the hidden number. Multiply if the parent is hidden. Divide if a child is hidden. Memorize the members of each fact family.

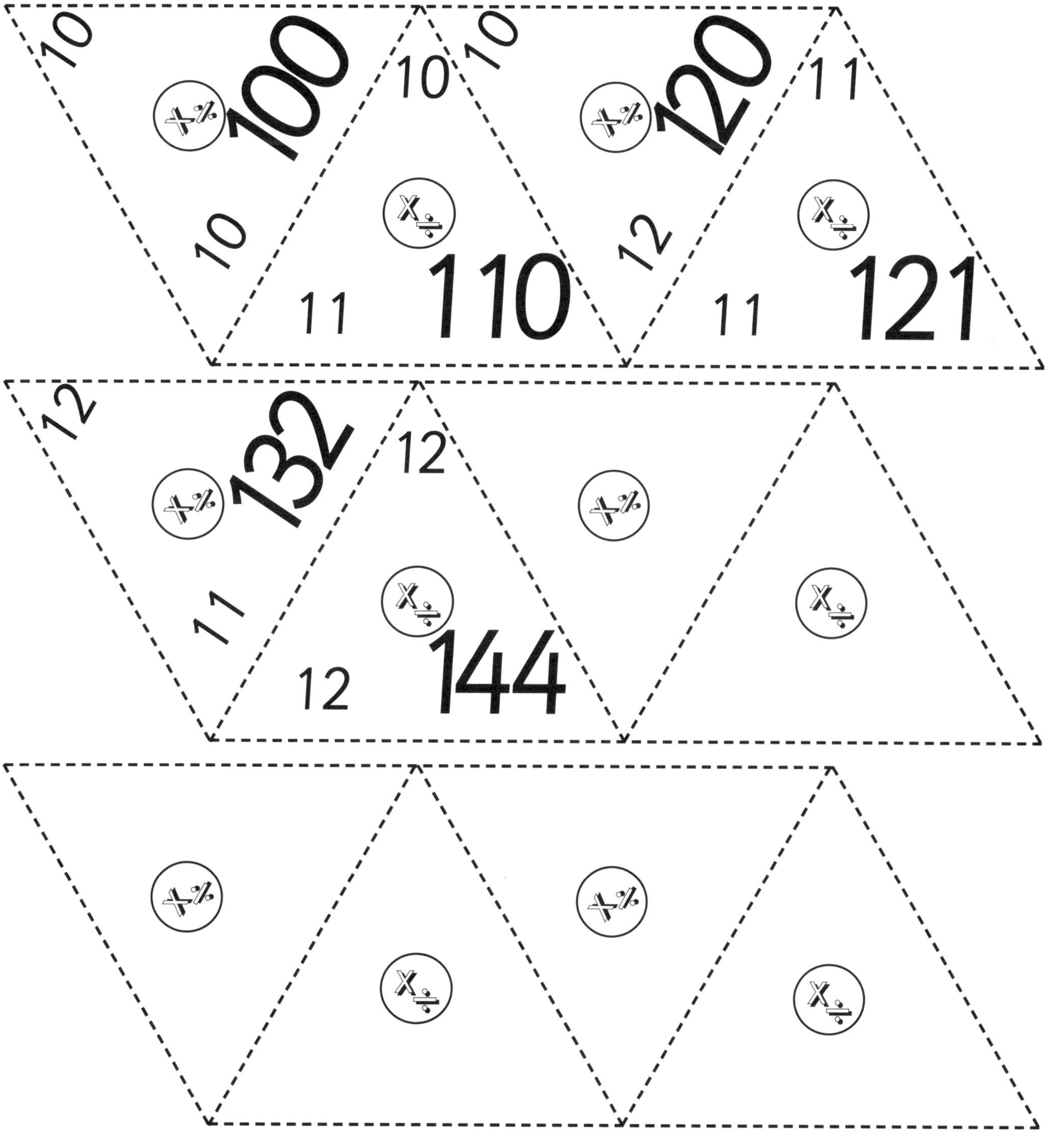

Name________________________

multiplication/division

Lizard's Challenge

Two is the smallest child in these multiplication and division fact families.

2 • 2 • 4   2 • 3 • 6   2 • 4 • 8   2 • 5 • 10

2 • 6 • 12   2 • 7 • 14   2 • 8 • 16   2 • 9 • 18

2 • 10 • 20   2 • 11 • 22   2 • 12 • 24

Solve each math sentence using the fact families above.

1. $\begin{array}{r} 2 \\ \underline{\times 6} \end{array}$

2. $12\overline{)24}$

3. $2\overline{)20}$

4. $\begin{array}{r} 9 \\ \underline{\times 2} \end{array}$

5. $\begin{array}{r} 11 \\ \underline{\times\ 2} \end{array}$

6. $2\overline{)10}$

7. $6\overline{)12}$

8. 6 x 2 =

9. 2 x 3 =

10. 7 x 2 =

11. $4\overline{)8}$

12. 2 x 9 =

13. $7\overline{)14}$

14. 12 x 2 =

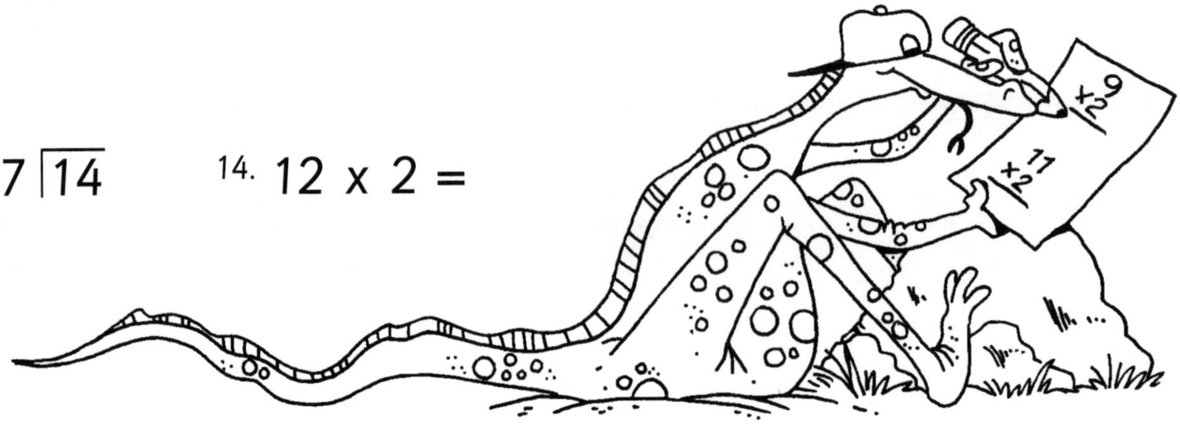

Sizzling CDs

Name______________________

multiplication/division

Fill in the missing numbers in these multiplication and division fact families.

1. 2•2•____
2. 2•____•6
3. 2•4•____
4. 2•____•10
5. 2•____•12
6. ____•7•14
7. 2•____•16
8. ____•9•18
9. 2•____•20
10. 2•____•22
11. 2•12•____

Use a multiplication or division problem to answer these story problems. Answer the questions with a complete sentence.

12. The music store had a two-for-one sale. They offered a special price on compact discs by 2 artists in each of these categories: popular, rock, jazz, country, rap, and gospel. Altogether, how many different CDs were on sale?

13. Zach received a gift certificate for CDs on his birthday. He browsed and found 8 different CDs by each of his 2 favorite groups. How many CDs was he interested in buying?

14. Ashley's music teacher bought 2 CDs by each of these composers: Bach, Beethoven, Chopin, Mozart, Haydn, Stravinsky, Rachmaninoff, Tchaikovsky, Wagner, and Saint-Saëns. How many CDs did she purchase altogether?

15. Jason bought 9 CD singles for $2.00 each. How much money did he spend?

Name____________________

multiplication/division

Thrilling Threes

Three is the smallest child in these multiplication and division fact families.

3 • 3 • 9   3 • 4 • 12   3 • 5 • 15

3 • 6 • 18   3 • 7 • 21   3 • 8 • 24   3 • 9 • 27

3 • 10 • 30   3 • 11 • 33   3 • 12 • 36

Refer to the fact families above to solve these equations.

1. $\begin{array}{r} 3 \\ \times\ 8 \\ \hline \end{array}$
2. $\begin{array}{r} 12 \\ \times\ 3 \\ \hline \end{array}$
3. $\begin{array}{r} 3 \\ \times\ 6 \\ \hline \end{array}$
4. $\begin{array}{r} 7 \\ \times\ 3 \\ \hline \end{array}$
5. $\begin{array}{r} 3 \\ \times\ 7 \\ \hline \end{array}$

6. 9 x 3 = _____
7. 8 x 3 = _____
8. 4 x 3 = _____
9. 3 x 3 = _____

10. $\begin{array}{r} 5 \\ \times\ 3 \\ \hline \end{array}$
11. $\begin{array}{r} 3 \\ \times\ 6 \\ \hline \end{array}$
12. $\begin{array}{r} 10 \\ \times\ 3 \\ \hline \end{array}$
13. $\begin{array}{r} 11 \\ \times\ 3 \\ \hline \end{array}$
14. $\begin{array}{r} 12 \\ \times\ 3 \\ \hline \end{array}$

15. $12\overline{)36}$
16. $3\overline{)33}$
17. $10\overline{)30}$
18. $3\overline{)27}$
19. $6\overline{)18}$

Name________________________

multiplication/division

My Future

For each fact family, write two multiplication and two division problems.

1. 3 • 4 • 12

X ____ X ____

2. 3 • 5 • 15

X ____ X ____

3. 3 • 7 • 21

X ____ X ____

4. 3 • 8 • 24

X ____ X ____

5. 3 • 10 • 30

X ____ X ____

Name____________________

multiplication/division

Fun-Damental Fours

Four is the smallest child in these fact families.

4 • 4 • 16	4 • 5 • 20	4 • 6 • 24
4 • 7 • 28	4 • 8 • 32	4 • 9 • 36
4 • 10 • 40	4 • 11 • 44	4 • 12 • 48

Refer to the fact families above to solve these equations.

1. 4 x 6 = ____
2. 6 x 4 = ____
3. 4 x 8 = ____
4. 8 x 4 = ____
5. 4 x 9 = ____
6. 9 x 4 = ____
7. 24 ÷ 4 = ____
8. 32 ÷ 4 = ____
9. 24 ÷ 6 = ____
10. 32 ÷ 8 = ____
11. 36 ÷ 4 = ____
12. 36 ÷ 9 = ____
13. 12 x 4 = ____
14. 4 x 12 = ____
15. 4 x 11 = ____
16. 11 x 4 = ____
17. 10 x 4 = ____
18. 4 x 10 = ____
19. 40 ÷ 4 = ____
20. 40 ÷ 10 = ____
21. 48 ÷ 4 = ____
22. 48 ÷ 12 = ____
23. 44 ÷ 4 = ____
24. 44 ÷ 11 = ____
25. 4 x 7 = ____
26. 4 x 5 = ____
27. 4 x 4 = ____
28. 4 x 9 = ____

String-a-Bead

Name____________________

multiplication/division

Fill in the missing numbers in these multiplication and division fact families.

1. 4•4•____
2. 4•____•20
3. 4•6•____
4. 4•____•28
5. 4•____•32
6. ____•9•36
7. 4•____•40
8. ____•11•44
9. 4•____•48

The fourth grade art class did a bead project. They used packs of beads with four in each. Answer each story problem below using multiplication and division facts.

10. Casey chose to make a bead necklace. The necklace required 48 beads. How many packs of beads did she need?

11. Phil decided to make a beaded key chain. The key chain required 8 packs of beads. How many beads were needed to make the key chain?

12. Dillon chose to make a Native American dream catcher. He selected and used 2 packs of red beads, 2 packs of tan beads, and 1 pack of gold. How many beads did he use in all?

13. Jackson wanted to make a zipper-pull for his backpack. His project required 44 beads altogether. How many packs should the teacher give him?

Name____________________

multiplication/division

Skating to Success

Five and six are the smallest children in these fact families.

5 • 5 • 25   5 • 6 • 30   5 • 7 • 35   5 • 8 • 40

5 • 9 • 45   5 • 10 • 50   5 • 11 • 55   5 • 12 • 60

Refer to the fact families above to solve.

1. 6×5
2. 11×5
3. 9×5
4. 5×7
5. 5×12
6. 5×5
7. 5×10
8. 9×5
9. 5×11
10. 5×8
11. $6 \overline{)30}$
12. $10 \overline{)50}$
13. $5 \overline{)45}$
14. $12 \overline{)60}$
15. $9 \overline{)45}$
16. $11 \overline{)55}$
17. $5 \overline{)35}$
18. $5 \overline{)55}$
19. $8 \overline{)40}$
20. $5 \overline{)25}$

Name_______________________

multiplication/division

Karate Class

A local sports club offered students an introductory workshop in karate. Teachers did demonstrations of the moves, then invited one child at a time for 5 minutes of personal instruction. Determine how long each teacher spent on individual instruction by multiplying the number of students by 5 minutes. The first one is done for you.

1. Session A: The first teacher demonstrated the front stance, the back stance, and the half-moon stance. Five students participated in the individual instruction session with the teacher.

   5 x 5 = 25 minutes

2. Session B: The next teacher demonstrated the cat stance, the hour-glass stance, and the rising block. Eight students participated in the individual instruction session with the teacher.

3. Session C: The first teacher returned to demonstrate the downward block, the knife-hand block, and the sweeping block. Twelve students had individual lessons.

4. Session D: Another instructor showed the inside wedge block, the front punch, and the lunge punch. Eleven students participated.

5. Session E: The teacher demonstrated the cat stance, the reverse punch, and the rising block to a group of nine students.

6. Session F: One of the teachers presented the reverse punch and the leading-hand jab. Six students participated in this lesson.

7. Session G: A visiting teacher displayed the three-punch combination and the half-punch. Ten students watched and then practiced with the teacher.

© Instructional Fair • TS Denison

Name____________________

multiplication/division

X Marks the Spot

Six, seven, and eight are the smallest children in these fact families.

6 • 6 • 36	6 • 7 • 42	6 • 8 • 48	6 • 9 • 54
6 • 10 • 60	6 • 11 • 66	6 • 12 • 72	7 • 7 • 49
7 • 8 • 56	7 • 9 • 63	7 • 10 • 70	7 • 11 • 77
7 • 12 • 84	8 • 8 • 64	8 • 9 • 72	8 • 10 • 80
8 • 11 • 88	8 • 12 • 96		

Refer to the fact families above to help fill in the missing numbers in the fact families. As you use the numbers in the box below, cross them out.

1. 6 • ____ • 60
2. ____ • 12 • 72
3. 7 • 11 • ____
4. ____ • 8 • 56
5. 7 • ____ • 70
6. 6 • 7 • ____
7. 6 • 6 • ____
8. ____ • 11 • 66
9. 8 • 8 • ____
10. ____ • 10 • 80
11. 8 • ____ • 96
12. ____ • 9 • 63
13. 6 • ____ • 48
14. 7 • 12 • ____
15. 6 • ____ • 54
16. 7 • 7 • ____

10	6	10	9	7	8	7	42
8	12	49	36	64	77	84	6

Name________________________

multiplication/division

A Video Business

Ashley's uncle owned a video store and often gave her copies of the older and less popular movies. She had an idea. Why not learn about business and set up a video rental for her friends? She made a flyer on her computer and gave it to her classmates.

Ashley's Video Rentals

Rent your movies for only $1.00 per tape!

Keep your movies for one whole week!

Get 'em Cheaper Keep 'em Longer!

Ashley's business was a success. In the first week, 6 people rented 6 movies each! How many movies did she rent altogether?

$$\begin{array}{rl} 6 & \text{people} \\ \times\ 6 & \text{movies} \\ \hline 36 & \text{rentals} \end{array}$$

Multiply to see how many movies she would rent in these situations.

1. 9 people x 8 movies rentals	2. 11 people x 7 movies rentals	3. 8 people x 8 movies rentals	4. 9 people x 6 movies rentals
5. 10 people x 6 movies rentals	6. 12 people x 6 movies rentals	7. 12 people x 8 movies rentals	8. 7 people x 6 movies rentals
9. 9 people x 7 movies rentals	10. 10 people x 8 movies rentals	11. 8 people x 7 movies rentals	12. 11 people x 8 movies rentals

Name________________________

multiplication/division

Goodies at the Movies

Nine, ten, eleven, and twelve are the smallest children in these fact families.

9 • 9 • 81   9 • 10 • 90   9 • 11 • 99   9 • 12 • 108

10 • 10 • 100   10 • 11 • 110   10 • 12 • 120

11 • 11 • 121   11 • 12 • 132

12 • 12 • 144

Refer to the fact families above to solve.

1. 100 ÷ 10 = ____
2. 12 x 9 = ____
3. 10 x 9 = ____
4. 121 ÷ 11 = ____
5. 132 ÷ 12 = ____
6. 11 x 9 = ____
7. 11 x 10 = ____
8. 108 ÷ 9 = ____
9. 10 x 12 = ____
10. 9 x 9 = ____
11. 11 x 11 = ____
12. 81 ÷ 9 = ____
13. 99 ÷ 11 = ____
14. 10 x 10 = ____
15. 90 ÷ 9 = ____
16. 120 ÷ 10 = ____
17. 110 ÷ 10 = ____
18. 11 x 12 = ____
19. 144 ÷ 12 = ____
20. 9 x 11 = ____

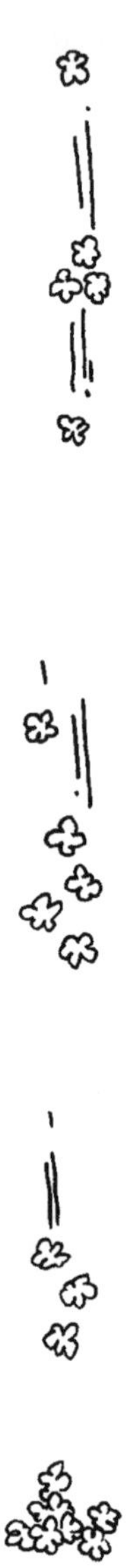

© Instructional Fair • TS Denison

Name________________________

multiplication/division

Bean Bag Buddies

Solve these problems using the fact families.

1. $12\overline{)108}$

2. $12\overline{)132}$

3. $12\overline{)144}$

4. $9\overline{)99}$

5. $11\overline{)99}$

6. $11\overline{)110}$

7. $10\overline{)120}$

8. $9\overline{)81}$

9. $10\overline{)90}$

10. $9\overline{)90}$

11. $\begin{array}{r} 9 \\ \underline{\times\ 9} \end{array}$

12. $\begin{array}{r} 10 \\ \underline{\times\ 10} \end{array}$

13. $\begin{array}{r} 11 \\ \underline{\times\ 9} \end{array}$

14. $\begin{array}{r} 12 \\ \underline{\times\ 11} \end{array}$

15. $\begin{array}{r} 12 \\ \underline{\times\ 10} \end{array}$

16. $\begin{array}{r} 10 \\ \underline{\times\ 9} \end{array}$

17. $\begin{array}{r} 11 \\ \underline{\times\ 10} \end{array}$

18. $\begin{array}{r} 9 \\ \underline{\times\ 11} \end{array}$

19. $\begin{array}{r} 11 \\ \underline{\times\ 11} \end{array}$

20. $\begin{array}{r} 10 \\ \underline{\times\ 11} \end{array}$

21. $\begin{array}{r} 12 \\ \underline{\times\ 12} \end{array}$

22. $\begin{array}{r} 12 \\ \underline{\times\ 9} \end{array}$

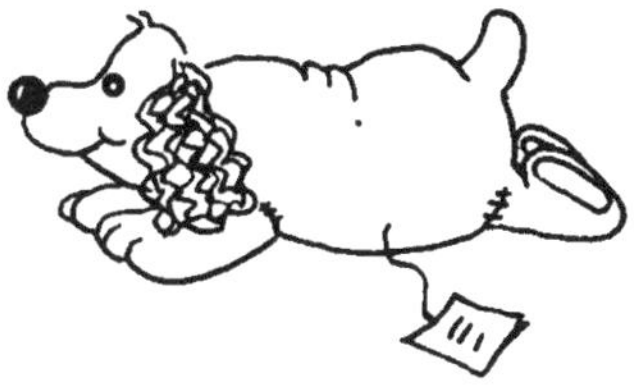

23. $100 \div 10 =$ ____

24. $121 \div 11 =$ ____

25. $81 \div 9 =$ ____

Name________________________

multiplication/division

Tricky Nines

You remember seeing nine in fact families. Here is a trick to help you recall these families.

Trick 1: Notice that the tens place of the parent is always one less than the smallest child.

2 • 9 • 18   5 • 9 • 45   8 • 9 • 72   4 • 9 • 36

Trick 2: Notice that the digits within the parent always add up to nine.

In the family	In the family	In the family
3 • 9 • 27	6 • 9 • 54	7 • 9 • 63
the parent 27 becomes	the parent 54 becomes	the parent 63 becomes
2 + 7 = 9	5 + 4 = 9	6 + 3 = 9

Put It Together: Use your knowledge of the nine tricks to solve 8 • 9 • ____

Trick 1: The tens place of the parent is one less than the smallest child.
8 is the smallest child, so the tens digit of the parent is 7.

Trick 2: In the nines family, the digits of the parent always add up to nine.
Since you know the tens digit is 7, solve 7 + __ = 9.
Since the answer is 2, put them together and the answer is 72.

Fill in the blanks below. Use the tricks above to help.

1. 5 • 9 • ____ One less than 5 is ____, so the tens digit in the parent will be ____.
   ____ + ____ = 9, therefore the fact family is ______________.
2. 7 • 9 • ____ One less than 7 is ____, so the tens digit in the parent will be ____.
   Therefore, the fact family is ______________.
3. 2 • 9 • ____ One less than 2 is ____. Therefore, the fact family is ______________.
4. 6 • 9 • ____ One less than 6 is ____. Therefore, the fact family is ______________.

Name________________________

multiplication/division

Chart What You've Learned II

Keep track of the facts you know. Notice the children are outside the chart and the parents are inside. Follow the column and row to match two children and write in the parent. You will notice the same family is found twice on the chart. That is because 3 x 4 and 4 x 3, both come from the same family. Once you know the family, you will know the answers to two multiplication problems.

Match the children and write in the parent for each of these families. The 3 • 4 • 12 family is done for you.

x	2	3	4	5	6	7	8	9	10	11	12
2											
3			12								
4		12									
5											
6											
7											
8											
9											
10											
11											
12											

Name________________________

multiplication/division

Art Supplies

Solve each problem. Color the blocks as directed.

If the smallest child is

3, 7, or 9, color the block red.

4 or 8, color the block blue.

5 or 10, color the block green.

6 or 11, color the block yellow.

1. 3 x 10	2. 4 x 8	3. 5 x 5	4. 9 x 6	5. 7 x 7
6. 3 x 6	7. 7 x 4	8. 11 x 8	9. 5 x 7	10. 6 x 6
11. 7 x 9	12. 3 x 12	13. 4 x 9	14. 9 x 5	15. 9 x 3
16. 4 x 4	17. 12 x 5	18. 6 x 9	19. 10 x 11	20. 8 x 9
21. 10 x 5	22. 10 x 10	23. 11 x 9	24. 12 x 11	25. 12 x 10

© Instructional Fair • TS Denison

Name________________________

multiplication/division

Getting in Shape

Solve each math fact. Name the fact family. Remember, always put the smallest child first, the bigger child second, and the parent last.

Example:

$$\begin{array}{r} 5 \\ \underline{\times\ 3} \\ 15 \end{array}$$

3 • 5 • 15

1. $\begin{array}{r} 6 \\ \underline{\times\ 7} \end{array}$ 6 • 7 • 42

2. $\begin{array}{r} 7 \\ \underline{\times\ 3} \end{array}$ ___•___•___

3. $\begin{array}{r} 4 \\ \underline{\times\ 3} \end{array}$ ___•___•___

4. 8 ⟌32 ___•___•___

5. 9 ⟌54 ___•___•___

6. 4 ⟌28 ___•___•___

7. $\begin{array}{r} 9 \\ \underline{\times\ 9} \end{array}$ ___•___•___

8. $\begin{array}{r} 8 \\ \underline{\times\ 9} \end{array}$ ___•___•___

9. $\begin{array}{r} 3 \\ \underline{\times\ 6} \end{array}$ ___•___•___

10. 6 ⟌48 ___•___•___

11. 9 ⟌63 ___•___•___

12. 7 ⟌49 ___•___•___

13. $\begin{array}{r} 7 \\ \underline{\times\ 8} \end{array}$ ___•___•___

14. $\begin{array}{r} 6 \\ \underline{\times\ 4} \end{array}$ ___•___•___

15. $\begin{array}{r} 4 \\ \underline{\times\ 6} \end{array}$ ___•___•___

© Instructional Fair • TS Denison

Name______________________

multiplication/division

Algebra Works

Using the fact families, solve for the X.

1. $3 \times X = 27$ X = ____

2. $8 \times X = 72$ X = ____

3. $X \times 6 = 24$ X = ____

4. $X \times 7 = 42$ X = ____

5. $8 \times 7 = X$ X = ____

6. $6 \times X = 36$ X = ____

7. $5 \times X = 15$ X = ____

8. $8 \times 8 = X$ X = ____

9. $10 \times X = 60$ X = ____

10. $X \times 5 = 45$ X = ____

11. $4 \times X = 44$ X = ____

12. $X \times 7 = 21$ X = ____

13. $8 \times X = 96$ X = ____

14. $9 \times X = 81$ X = ____

15. $X \times 3 = 24$ X = ____

16. $11 \times X = 121$ X = ____

17. $X \times 5 = 40$ X = ____

18. $X \times 9 = 36$ X = ____

© Instructional Fair • TS Denison

Name____________________

multiplication/division

Full Steam Ahead

Fact families can be found in larger math problems. To solve, begin with the ones column.

+2 45 x 4 0	Remember the math fact family 4 • 5 • 20. Carry the two.

+2 45 x 4 180	Remember the math fact family 4 • 4 • 16. Add the 2 you carried.

Solve these multiplication problems. Name the fact families found in each.

1. 98 x 6 ___•___•___ ___•___•___

2. 19 x 9 ___•___•___ ___•___•___

3. 97 x 7 ___•___•___ ___•___•___

4. 57 x 5 ___•___•___ ___•___•___

5. 98 x 8 ___•___•___ ___•___•___

6. 59 x 4 ___•___•___ ___•___•___

7. 45 x 3 ___•___•___ ___•___•___

8. 76 x 6 ___•___•___ ___•___•___

9. 48 x 5 ___•___•___ ___•___•___

10. 63 x 4 ___•___•___ ___•___•___

11. 76 x 3 ___•___•___ ___•___•___

12. 98 x 3 ___•___•___ ___•___•___

Answer Key

Math Fact Families **4**

Circle the following:

1. 7 + 8 = 15 (vertical and horizontal)
2. 7 + 6 = 13, 13 – 6 = 7
3. 8 + 9 = 17, 17 – 9 = 8
4. 8 + 6 = 14, 14 – 6 = 8

Look to the Parent **5**

1. circle 14, +
2. circle 14, +
3. circle 14, –
4. circle 14, –
5. circle 14, +
6. circle 14, +
7. circle 14, –
8. circle 14, –

Soaring Through Threes **9**

1. 3 • 3 • 6
2. 3 • 8 • 11
3. 3 • 5 • 8
4. 3 • 4 • 7
5. 3 • 7 • 10
6. 3 • 6 • 9
7. 3 • 9 • 12

Fours All the Way **10**

1. 4 • 4 • 8
2. 4 • 9 • 13
3. 4 • 7 • 11
4. 4 • 6 • 10
5. 4 • 5 • 9
6. 4 • 8 • 12

It's a Fact **11**

~~6~~	~~5~~	8	6	~~6~~	~~5~~	4	1	~~5~~	2	~~6~~	4	~~5~~	11	7
6	~~8~~	~~6~~	4	3	~~7~~	~~5~~	3	9	~~8~~	7	~~7~~	1	~~9~~	6
3	7	~~14~~	~~11~~	~~5~~	1	~~13~~	~~10~~	2	9	~~13~~	2	~~13~~	2	~~14~~
~~5~~	7	~~6~~	0	0	~~7~~	6	7	0	0	7	1	~~5~~	9	3
6	~~5~~	4	~~8~~	6	5	~~12~~	~~6~~	1	~~5~~	8	1	4	~~8~~	3
6	3	~~10~~	5	~~14~~	2	3	2	~~6~~	4	~~6~~	9	~~5~~	4	~~13~~
1	6	9	6	7	7	1	8	9	~~12~~	3	~~11~~	1	~~9~~	0
7	~~5~~	1	9	8	4	~~6~~	5	8	6	4	5	~~6~~	2	~~14~~
6	9	~~7~~	2	0	3	5	~~6~~	5	7	9	0	9	~~9~~	7
9	0	6	~~12~~	3	1	9	1	~~12~~	8	2	14	4	4	~~15~~

Surfing Through 7, 8, and 9 ....**12**

1. 15
2. 14
3. 8
4. 9
5. 18
6. 17
7. 7
8. 7
9. 16
10. 16
11. 8
12. 8
13. 15
14. 14
15. 9
16. 8
17. 16
18. 17
19. 7
20. 9

Focus on the Bigger Picture **14**

1. 77, 3 • 4 • 7
2. 32, 2 • 6 • 8, 3 • 3 • 6
3. 99, 4 • 5 • 9
4. 43, 3 • 3 • 6, 4 • 4 • 8
5. 88, 3 • 5 • 8
6. 53, 3 • 5 • 8
7. 56, 3 • 6 • 9, 4 • 5 • 9
8. 43, 3 • 4 • 7
9. 52, 2 • 7 • 9, 4 • 5 • 9

Climbing Higher **15**

1. 81, 3 • 8 • 11, 3 • 4 • 7
2. 102, 5 • 7 • 12, 3 • 6 • 9
3. 100, 5 • 5 • 10, 4 • 5 • 9
4. 91, 3 • 8 • 11, 4 • 4 • 8
5. 94, 5 • 9 • 14, 3 • 5 • 8
6. 73, 5 • 8 • 13, 3 • 3 • 6
7. 93, 6 • 7 • 13, 4 • 4 • 8
8. 91, 4 • 7 • 11, 3 • 5 • 8
9. 95, 7 • 8 • 15, 3 • 5 • 8

Diving for Knowledge **16**

1. 53, 3 • 8 • 11, 3 • 5 • 8
2. 38, 7 • 8 • 15, 3 • 3 • 6
3. 39, 5 • 9 • 14, 3 • 5 • 8
4. 38, 3 • 8 • 11, 3 • 4 • 7
5. 38, 5 • 8 • 13, 3 • 3 • 6
6. 55, 5 • 5 • 10, 3 • 5 • 8
7. 39, 7 • 9 • 16, 3 • 4 • 7
8. 40, 0 • 2 • 2, 3 • 4 • 7
9. 55, 5 • 7 • 12, 3 • 5 • 8

Facts in Dollars and Decimals **17**

1. $8.79
2. $26.55
3. $21.43
4. $10.03
5. $10.51
6. $89.46
7. $67.48
8. $76.76
9. $6.12
10. $18.10
11. $1.64
12. $0.13
13. $8.13
14. $9.69
15. $2.22
16. $2.42

Starting with Algebra **18**

1. 3
2. 3
3. 9
4. 6
5. 9
6. 4
7. 7
8. 5
9. 4
10. 7
11. 4
12. 9
13. 8
14. 5
15. 8
16. 3
17. 10
18. 3
19. 3
20. 8

Answer Key

Algebra Expert 19

1. 0	2. 4	3. 5	4. 5
5. 4	6. 6	7. 6	8. 9
9. 4	10. 14	11. 6	12. 7
13. 8	14. 9	15. 3	16. 7
17. 6	18. 13	19. 6	20. 9

Multiplying and Dividing Fact Families 20

Circle the following:

1. 8 x 2 = 16, 16 ÷ 2 = 8
2. 5 ÷ 1 = 5 (vertical and horizontal)
3. 24 ÷ 6 = 4
4. 8 x 6 = 48, 48 ÷ 8 = 6

Look to the Parent II 21

1. 12	2. 12	3. 21	4. 28
5. 20	6. 24	7. 18	8. 36
9. 12	10. 20	11. 12	12. 21
13. 20	14. 24	15. 18	16. 36

Lizard's Challenge 28

1. 12	2. 2	3. 10	4. 18
5. 22	6. 5	7. 2	8. 12
9. 6	10. 14	11. 2	12. 18
13. 2	14. 24		

Sizzling CDs 29

1. 4	2. 3	3. 8	4. 5
5. 6	6. 2	7. 8	8. 2
9. 10	10. 11	11. 24	

12. 2 x 6 = 12 CDs
13. 2 x 8 = 16 CDs
14. 2 x 10 = 20 CDs
15. $2.00 x 9 = $18.00 spent

Thrilling Threes 30

1. 24	2. 36	3. 18	4. 21
5. 21	6. 27	7. 24	8. 12
9. 9	10. 15	11. 18	12. 30
13. 33	14. 36	15. 3	16. 11
17. 3	18. 9	19. 3	

My Future 31

1. 3 x 4 = 12, 4 x 3 = 12
   12 ÷ 3 = 4, 12 ÷ 4 = 3
2. 3 x 5 = 15, 5 x 3 = 15
   15 ÷ 3 = 5, 15 ÷ 5 = 3
3. 3 x 7 = 21, 7 x 3 = 21
   21 ÷ 3 = 7, 21 ÷ 7 = 3
4. 3 x 8 = 24, 8 x 3 = 24
   24 ÷ 3 = 8, 24 ÷ 8 = 3
5. 3 x 10 = 30, 10 x 3 = 30
   30 ÷ 3 = 10, 30 ÷ 10 = 3

Fun-Damental Fours 32

1. 24	2. 24	3. 32	4. 32
5. 36	6. 36	7. 6	8. 8
9. 4	10. 4	11. 9	12. 4
13. 48	14. 48	15. 44	16. 44
17. 40	18. 40	19. 10	20. 4
21. 12	22. 4	23. 11	24. 4
25. 28	26. 20	27. 16	28. 36

String-a-Bead 33

1. 16	2. 5	3. 24	4. 7
5. 8	6. 4	7. 10	8. 4

9. 12
10. 48 ÷ 4 = 12 packs
11. 8 x 4 = 32 beads
12. 5 x 4 = 20 beads
13. 44 ÷ 4 = 11 packs

Skating to Success 34

1. 30	2. 55	3. 45
4. 35	5. 60	6. 25
7. 50	8. 45	9. 55
10. 40	11. 5	12. 5
13. 9	14. 5	15. 5
16. 5	17. 7	18. 11
19. 5	20. 5	

Karate Class 35

1. 5 x 5 = 25 minutes
2. 8 x 5 = 40 minutes
3. 12 x 5 = 60 minutes
4. 11 x 5 = 55 minutes
5. 9 x 5 = 45 minutes
6. 6 x 5 = 30 minutes
7. 10 x 5 = 50 minutes

X Marks the Spot 36

1. 10	2. 6	3. 77	4. 7
5. 10	6. 42	7. 36	8. 6
9. 64	10. 8	11. 12	12. 7
13. 8	14. 84	15. 9	16. 49

A Video Business 37

1. 72	2. 77	3. 64
4. 54	5. 60	6. 72
7. 96	8. 42	9. 63
10. 80	11. 56	12. 88

Answer Key

Goodies at the Movies **38**

1. 10	2. 108	3. 90	4. 11
5. 11	6. 99	7. 110	8. 12
9. 120	10. 81	11. 121	12. 9
13. 9	14. 100	15. 10	16. 12
17. 11	18. 132	19. 12	20. 99

Bean Bag Buddies **39**

1. 9	2. 11	3. 12	4. 11
5. 9	6. 10	7. 12	8. 9
9. 9	10. 10	11. 81	12. 100
13. 99	14. 132	15. 120	16. 90
17. 110	18. 99	19. 121	20. 110
21. 144	22. 108	23. 10	24. 11
25. 9			

Tricky Nines **40**

1. 45, 4, 4, 4 + 5 = 9, 5 • 9 • 45
2. 63, 6, 6, 7 • 9 • 63
3. 18, 1, 2 • 9 • 18
4. 54, 5, 6 • 9 • 54

Art Supplies **42**

1. 30, red	2. 32, blue
3. 25, green	4. 54, yellow
5. 49, red	6. 18, red
7. 28, blue	8. 88, blue
9. 35, green	10. 36, yellow
11. 63, red	12. 36, red
13. 36, blue	14. 45, green
15. 27, red	16. 16, blue
17. 60, green	18. 54, yellow
19. 110, green	20. 72, blue
21. 50, green	22. 100, green
23. 99, red	24. 132, yellow
25. 120, green	

Getting in Shape **43**

1. 42, 6 • 7 • 42	2. 21, 3 • 7 • 21
3. 12, 3 • 4 • 12	4. 4, 4 • 8 • 32
5. 6, 6 • 9 • 54	6. 7, 4 • 7 • 28
7. 81, 9 • 9 • 81	8. 72, 8 • 9 • 72
9. 18, 3 • 6 • 18	10. 8, 6 • 8 • 48
11. 7, 7 • 9 • 63	12. 7, 7 • 7 • 49
13. 56, 7 • 8 • 56	14. 24, 4 • 6 • 24
15. 24, 4 • 6 • 24	

Algebra Works **44**

1. 9	2. 9	3. 4	4. 6
5. 56	6. 6	7. 3	8. 64
9. 6	10. 9	11. 11	12. 3
13. 12	14. 9	15. 8	16. 11
17. 8	18. 4		

Full Steam Ahead **45**

1. 588, 6 • 8 • 48, 6 • 9 • 54
2. 171, 9 • 9 • 81, 1 • 9 • 9
3. 679, 7 • 7 • 49, 7 • 9 • 63
4. 285, 5 • 7 • 35, 5 • 5 • 25
5. 784, 8 • 8 • 64, 8 • 9 • 72
6. 236, 4 • 9 • 36, 4 • 5 • 20
7. 135, 3 • 5 • 15, 3 • 4 • 12
8. 456, 6 • 6 • 36, 6 • 7 • 42
9. 240, 5 • 8 • 40, 4 • 5 • 20
10. 252, 3 • 4 • 12, 4 • 6 • 24
11. 228, 3 • 6 • 18, 3 • 7 • 21
12. 294, 3 • 8 • 24, 3 • 9 • 27

© Instructional Fair • TS Denison